Dear Daddy,

Thanks for being the first Gandhian philosopher in my life (although I didn't realize it.

You are an amazing father, husband, and someone I respect so deeply.

Love always, Sima :)

Quotes of Gandhi

Quotes

of

Gandhi

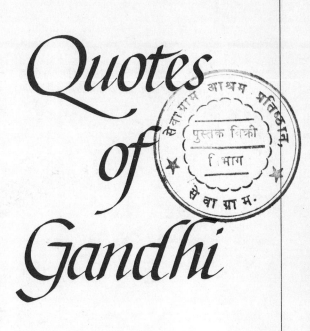

GANDHI BOOK CENTRE
Bombay Sarvodaya Mandal
299, Tardeo Raod, Nana Chowk
Bombay - 7 INDIA ✆ 387 2061
email:info@mkgandhi-sarvodaya.org
www.mkgandhi-sarvodaya.org

Compiled by Shalu Bhalla
41, Pali Hill, Bandra, Bombay.

Exclusive Distributors
UBS Publishers' Distributors Ltd.
5 Ansari Road, New Delhi-110 002

ISBN 81-85273-51-0

Price Rs.135

Foreword

"He was the kingliest of kings and more,
   He builded kingdoms and pulled
                              kingdoms down.
Nor ever cared himself to wear a crown,
   His shining nakedness was all he wore."

Evolution which travels smoothly along timelessness, at certain urgent points of its process, turns into a revolution which has the arcane quality of moulding, for its own nourishment and resuscitation, certain unique, singular, irreproducable phenomena in human forms that pass into history and the history of the Divine.

Such rare breathtaking beings are not born, but just happen. To name but a few

on the undying list of God, the deathless
ones on earth, whose influence passes into the
lives of generations in which they resurrect
keeping evolution alive: Ramakrishna
Paramahansa, Vivekananda, Anandamai,
Sri Aurobindo, Ramana Maharshi and
Gandhi, are the ripest contribution of Heaven
to earth. Without our being conscious of the
fact, they help millions, not only of our
country, but of the world, to continue to
breathe, dream, to ache for a shining world
yet in the making. They were all apostles of
peace, not merely of the peace as contrasted
by war, but the peace of Christ which passeth
all understanding.

　　With Gandhi, non-violence was never,
even for a fraction of a second, the weapon
of the weak, but always the weapon of the

strong. He was an ancestor come back, full of love and faith and naked simplicity of kindly thought, who would not have dreamt, even in a dream, of hurting a fly. The word revenge was never in Gandhi's dictionary.

Here is a book, which I strongly believe, should be found in every home, since it contains a world of wisdom. Specially today, when the younger generation seems to be unconsiously imbibing superficial thought. I can only hope that a study of these quotations will help to bridge and cancel wholly, not just this generation gap, but also this veneration gap.

Harendranath Chattopadhyaya

An eye for an eye only ends up making the whole world blind.

*Literary education
is of no value,
if it is not able
to build up
a sound character.*

1917

Woman
is the companion of man,
gifted with
equal mental capacities.
She has the right
to participate
in the minutest details
in the activities of man,
and she has an equal right
of freedom
and liberty with him.

1917

Hatred ever kills,
Love never dies
such is the vast difference
between the two.
What is obtained by love
is retained for all time.
What is obtained by hatred
proves a burden
in reality,
for it increases hatred.

1919

Fear of death
makes us devoid
both of valour and religion.
For want of valour
is want of religious faith.

1919

There are times
when you have to obey
a call which is
the highest of all,
i.e. the voice of conscience
even though such obedience
may cost many a bitter tear,
and even more,
separation from friends,
from family,
from the state
to which you may belong,
from all that you have held
as dear as life itself.
For this obedience
is the law of our being.

1919

Insistence on truth
can come into play
when one party practises
untruth or injustice.
Only then
can love be tested.
True friendship
is put to the test
only when one party disregards
the obligation of friendship.

1919

For me, the present is merged
in eternity,
I may not sacrifice
the latter for the present.

1919

The test of friendship
is assistance in adversity,
and that too,
unconditional assistance.
Co-operation
which needs consideration
is a commercial contract
and not friendship.
Conditional co-operation
is like adulterated cement
which does not bind.

1919

It may be long
before the law of love
will be recognised
in international affairs.
The machineries of government
stand between
and hide the hearts
of one people
from those of another.

1919

A vow
is a purely religious act
which cannot be taken
in a fit of passion.
It can be taken only
with a mind purified
and composed
and with God as witness.

1919

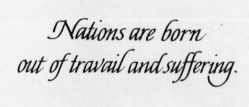

*Nations are born
out of travail and suffering.*

1920

*Religion
is a matter of the heart.
No physical inconvenience
can warrant abandonment
of one's own religion.*

1920

Non-cooperation is an attempt
to awaken the masses,
to a sense of their dignity
and power.
This can only be done
by enabling them to realize
that they need not fear
brute force,
if they would but know
the soul within.

1920

Public opinion alone can keep a society pure and healthy.

1920

Whenever I see an erring man,
I say to myself
I have also erred;
when I see a lustful man
I say to myself,
so was I once;
and in this way I feel kinship
with everyone in the world
and feel
that I cannot be happy without
the humblest of us being happy.

1920

To forgive is not to forget.
The merit lies in loving
in spite of the vivid knowledge
that the one that must be loved
is not a friend.
There is no merit
in loving an enemy
when you forget him for a friend.

1920

Strength does not come from physical capacity. It comes from an indomitable will.

1920

The moment there is suspicion
about a person's motives,
everything he does becomes tainted.

1920

Are creeds such simple things
like the clothes
which a man can change
at will and put on at will ?
Creeds are such for which
people live for ages and ages.

1921

I have but shadowed forth
my intense longing
to lose myself in the Eternal
and become
merely a lump of clay
in the Potter's divine hands
so that my service
may become more certain
because uninterrupted
by the baser self in me.

1921

An error does not become truth
by reason of
multiplied propagation,
nor does truth become error
because nobody will see it.

1921

A man who broods on evil
is as bad as a man who does evil,
if he is no worse.

1921

Suffering
cheerfully endured,
ceases to be suffering
and is transmuted
into an ineffable joy.

1921

As soon as we lose the moral basis,
we cease to be religious.
There is no such thing as religion
over-riding morality.
Man, for instance,
cannot be untruthful,
cruel or incontinent
and claim
to have God on his side.

1921

*Even as wisdom often comes
from the mouths of babes,
so does it often come
from the mouths of old people.
The golden rule is
to test everything
in the light of reason
and experience,
no matter from where it comes.*

1921

Non-cooperation is directed
not against men
but against measures.
It is not directed
against the Governors,
but against the system
they administer.
The roots of non-cooperation
lie not in hatred
but in justice,
if not in love.

1921

I do not want my house
to be walled in on all sides
and my windows to be stuffed.
I want the cultures of all the lands
to be blown about my house
as freely as possible.
But I refuse
to be blown off my feet by any.
I refuse to live
in other people's houses
as an interloper,
a beggar or a slave.

1921

Measures must always
in a progressive society
be held superior to men,
who are after all
imperfect instruments,
working for their fulfilment.

1921

I will far rather see
the race of man extinct
than that we should become
less than beasts
by making
the noblest of God's creation,
woman,
the object of our lust.

1921

The spirit of non-violence
necessarily leads to humility.
Non-violence means
reliance on God,
the rock of ages.
If we would seek his aid,
we must approach Him
with a humble and contrite heart.

1921

Abstract truth has no value
unless it incarnates
in human beings who represent it,
by proving their readiness
to die for it.

1921

I am a Puritan myself,
but I am catholic
towards others.

1921

There is a higher court
than courts of justice
and that is
the court of conscience.
It supercedes
all other courts.

1921

Non-cooperation is
beyond the reach of the bayonet.
It has found an abiding place
in the Indian heart.
Workers like me will go
when the hour has struck,
but non-cooperation will remain.

1921

Intolerance is itself
a form of violence
and an obstacle to the growth
of a true democratic spirit.

1921

This campaign of non-cooperation
has no reference to diplomacy,
secret or open.
The only diplomacy it admits of
is the statement and pursuance
of truth at any cost.

1921

God is,
even though
the whole world
deny him.
Truth stands,
even if there be
no public support.
It is self-sustained.

1922

*Never has man reached
his destination
by persistence in deviation
from the straight path.*

1922

I claim that human mind
or human society
is not divided
into watertight compartments
called social,
political and religious.
All act and react
upon one another.

1922

The only way
love punishes
is by suffering.

1922

The only virtue I want to claim
is truth and non-violence.
I lay no claim
to superhuman powers.
I want none.
I wear the same corruptible flesh
that the weakest of
my fellow beings wears,
and am therefore
as liable to err as any.
My services have many limitations,
but God has upto now
blessed them
in spite of the imperfections.

1922

The human voice
can never reach
the distance
that is covered by
the still small voice
of conscience.

1922.

If we want to cultivate
a true spirit of democracy
we cannot afford
to be intolerant.
Intolerance betrays
want of faith in one's cause.

1922

When I admire
the wonders of a sunset
or the beauty of the moon,
my soul expands
in the worship of the creator.

1924

Violent means
will give violent freedom.
That would be a menace
to the world
and to India herself.

1924

Religion is more than life.
Remember that his own religion
is the truest to every man
even if it stands low
in the scales of
philosophical comparison.

1924

In nature
there is fundamental unity
running through all
the diversity we see about us.
Religions are given to mankind
so as to accelerate
the process of realisation
of fundamental unity.

1924

*I believe in
absolute oneness of God
and therefore
also of humanity.*

1924

However
much I may sympathise with
and admire worthy motives,
I am an uncompromising
opponent
of violent methods
even to serve
the noblest of causes.

1924

Birth and death are not
two different states,
but they are different aspects
of the same state.
There is as little reason
to deplore the one
as there is
to be pleased over the other.

1924

*For me every ruler is alien
that defies public opinion.*

1924

Experience convinces me
that permanent good
can never be the outcome
of untruth & violence.
Even if my belief is
a fond delusion,
it will be admitted that
it is a fascinating delusion.

1924

I do not want to
foresee the future.
I am concerned
with taking care
of the present.
God has given me no control
over the moment following.

1924

Indeed one's faith
in one's plans and methods
is truly tested
when the horizon before one
is the blackest.

1924

*It is my own firm belief
that the strength of the soul
grows in proportion
as you subdue the flesh.*

1924

My trust is solely in God.
And I trust men
only because I trust God.
If I had no God to rely upon,
I should be like Timon,
a hater of my species.

1924

One's own religion is after all
a matter between oneself
and one's Maker
and no one else's.

1924

My religion is based on truth
and non-violence.
Truth is my God.
Non-violence is the means
of realising Him.

1925

It is any day better to stand erect
with a broken
and bandaged head
than to crawl on one's belly,
in order to be able
to save one's head.

1925

Better far than cowardice
is killing
and being killed in battle.

1925

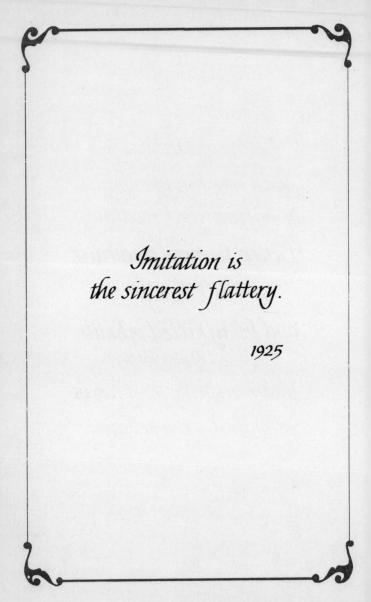

*Imitation is
the sincerest flattery.*

1925

Let no one charge me
with ever having abused
or encouraged weakness
or surrendered
on matters of principle.
But I have said,
as I say again,
that every trifle must not be
dignified into a principle.

1925

*Violent men
have not been known
in history to die to a man.
They die up to a point.*

1925

*Justice that love gives
is a surrender,
justice that law gives
is a punishment.*

1925

I am but a poor struggling soul
yearning to be wholly good,
wholly truthful
and wholly non-violent
in thought, word and deed;
but ever failing to reach the ideal
which I know to be true.
It is a painful climb,
but the pain of it is
a positive pleasure to me.
Each step upwards
makes me feel stronger
and fit for the next.

1925

*Moral authority
is never retained
by any attempt to hold on to it.
It comes without seeking
and is retained without effort.*

1925

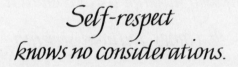

Self-respect
knows no considerations.

1925

Power is of two kinds.
One is obtained by
the fear of punishment
and the other by acts of love.
Power based on love is
a thousand times more effective
and permanent than the one
derived from fear of punishment .

1925

A religion
that takes no account
of practical affairs
and does not help to solve them
is no religion.

1925

*There is no principle
worth the name
if it is not wholly good.*

1925

No sacrifice is worth the name
unless it is a joy.
Sacrifice and a long face
go ill together.
Sacrifice is 'making sacred'.
He must be a poor specimen
of humanity
who is in need of sympathy
for his sacrifice.

1925

*That service is the noblest
which is rendered
for its own sake.*

1925

*Every formula of every religion
has in this age of reason,
to submit to the acid test
of reason and universal assent.*

1925

God tries his votaries
through and through
but never beyond endurance.
He gives them strength enough
to go through the ordeal
he prescribes for them.

1925

Love never claims,
it ever gives.
Love ever suffers,
never resents,
never revenges itself.

1925

I claim to be a simple individual
liable to err
like any other fellow mortal.
I own, however, that
I have humility enough to confess
my errors and to retrace my steps.

1926

Truth is by nature self-evident,
as soon as you remove
the cobwebs of ignorance
that surround it,
it shines clear.

1926

Adaptability is not imitation.
It means power of resistance
and assimilation.

1926

Man has reason, discrimination
and free-will such as it is.
The brute has no such thing.
It is not a free agent,
and knows no distinction
between virtue and vice,
good and evil.
Man, being a free agent,
knows these distinctions,
and when he follows
his higher nature,

shows himself far superior
to the brute,
but when he follows
his baser nature
can show himself lower
than the brute.

1926

Anger is the enemy of Ahimsa *
and pride is a monster
that swallows it up.

1926

*A principle is
the expression of perfection,
and as imperfect beings like us
cannot practise perfection,
we devise every moment limits
of its compromise in practice.*

1926

It is easy enough to say,
'I do not believe in God'.
For God permits all things
to be said of Him with impunity.
He looks at our acts.
And any breach of His Law
carries with it,
not its vindictive,
but its purifying,
compelling punishment.

1926

He who trifles with truth
cuts at the root of Ahimsa.
He who is angry
is guilty of Himsa.

1926

*Human society
is a ceaseless growth,
an unfoldment
in terms of spirituality.*

1926

If patience is worth anything,
it must endure to the end of time.
And a living faith will last
in the midst of
the blackest storm.

1926

Though we may know Him
by a thousand names,
He is one
and the same to us all.

1926

*I have found by experience
that man makes his plans
to be often upset by God,
but, at the same time,
where the ultimate goal is
the search of truth,
no matter how
a man's plans are frustrated
the issue is never injurious
and often better
than anticipated.*

1927

A 'no' uttered
from deepest conviction
is better and greater
than a 'yes'
merely uttered to please,
or what is worse,
to avoid trouble.

1927

*Friendship that insists
upon agreement
on all matters
is not worth the name.
Friendship to be real
must ever sustain
the weight of honest differences,
however sharp they be.*

1927

A clean confession,
combined with a promise
never to commit the sin again,
when offered before one
who has the right to receive it,
is the purest type of repentance.

1927

Purity of personal life
is the one indispensable condition
for building up
a sound education.

1927

Perfection
is the exclusive attribute of God,
and it is indescribable,
untranslatable.
I do believe that it is possible
for human beings
to become perfect,
even as God is perfect.
It is necessary for all of us
to aspire after that perfection
but when that blessed state
is attained, it becomes
indescribable, indefinable.

1927

What is true of the individual
will be to-morrow true
of the whole nation
if individuals will but refuse
to lose heart and hope.

1927

Service which is rendered
without joy
helps neither the servant
nor the served.
But all other pleasures
and possessions
pale into nothingness
before service which is rendered
in a spirit of joy.

1927

*It has always been
a mystery to me
how men can feel
themselves honoured
by the humiliation
of their fellow beings.*

1927

The spirit of democracy
is not a mechanical thing
to be adjusted
by abolition of forms.
It requires change of heart.

1927

It is quite proper
to resist and attack a system,
but to resist
and attack its author
is tantamount to resisting
and attacking oneself, for we are all
tarred with the same brush,
and are children of
one and the same Creator, and as such
the divine powers within us are infinite.

To slight a single human being,
is to slight those divine powers and
thus to harm not only that Being,
but with Him, the whole world.

1927

*Let us all be brave enough
to die the death of a martyr,
but let no one lust for martyrdom.*

1927

A true soldier does not argue,
as he marches,
how success
is going to be ultimately achieved.
But he is confident that
if he only plays his humble part well,
somehow or other
the battle will be won.
It is in that spirit
that every one of us should act.
It is not given to us
to know the future.
But it is given to everyone of us
to know
how to do our own part well.

1927

If co-operation is a duty,
I hold that non-co-operation also
under certain conditions
is equally a duty.

1927

Of all the animal creation of God,
man is the only animal
who has been created
in order that
he may know his Maker.
Man's aim in life is not
therefore
to add from day to day
to his material prospects
and to his material possessions,
but his predominant calling is,
from day to day to come nearer
to his own Maker.

1927

Spiritual relationship
is far more precious than physical.
Physical relationship divorced
from spiritual
is body without soul.

1927

Man and his deed are
two distinct things.
Whereas a good deed should
call forth approbation
and a wicked deed dis-approbation,
the doer of the deed,
whether good or wicked
always deserves respect
or pity as the case may be.
Hate the sin and not the sinner
is a precept which
though easy enough to understand
is rarely practised, and that is why
the poison of hatred spreads
in the world.

All the religions of the world,
while they may differ
in other respects,
unitedly proclaim that
nothing lives in this world
but Truth.

1927

Morality is the basis of things
and truth is
the substance of all morality.

1927

Mankind is notoriously too dense
to read the signs
that God sends from time to time.

We require drums to be beaten
into our ears,
before we should wake
from our trance
and hear the warning
and see that to lose oneself in all,
is the only way to find oneself.

1927

*I do not want any patronage,
as I do not give any.
I am a lover of my own liberty,
and so I would do nothing
to restrict yours.
I simply want to please
my own conscience,
which is God.*

1927

Real suffering,
bravely borne,
melts even a heart of stone.
Such is the potency of suffering.
And there lies the key
to Satyagraha.

1928

*But for my faith in God,
I should have been
a raving maniac.*

1928

There is an orderliness
in the universe,
there is an unalterable law
governing everything
and every being
that exists or lives.
It is no blind law;
for no blind law
can govern the conduct
of living beings.

1928

The first condition
of humaneness
is a little humility
and a little diffidence
about the correctness
of one's conduct
and a little receptiveness.

1928

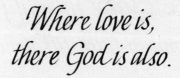

Where love is,
there God is also.

1928

*We are merely the instruments
of the Almighty's will
and therefore ignorant
of what helps us forward
and what acts
as an impediment.
We must thus rest satisfied
with the knowledge
only of the means
and if these are pure,
we can fearlessly leave the end
to take care of itself.*

1928

There will have to be
rigid and iron discipline
before we achieve
anything great and enduring,
and that discipline
will not come
by mere academic argument
and appeal to reason and logic.

Discipline is learnt
in the school of adversity

1928

Non-violence is not a quality
to be evolved
or expressed to order.
It is an inward growth
depending for sustenance
upon intense individual effort.

1928

Constant development
is the law of life,
and a man who always tries
to maintain his dogmas
in order to appear
consistent drives himself
into a false position.

1928

I believe that cunning is not only morally wrong but also politically inexpedient, and have therefore always discountenanced its use even from the practical standpoint.

1928

When anything assumes
the strength of a creed,
it becomes self-sustained
and derives the needed
support from within.

1928

I do dimly perceive
that whilst everything
around me is ever-changing,
ever-dying, there is underlying
all that change a living Power
that is changeless, that
holds all together, that
creates, dissolves and recreates.
That informing power
or spirit is God.
And since nothing else I see
merely through the senses
can or will persist, He alone is.

1928

Non-violence and cowardice
are contradictory terms.
Non-violence is

the greatest virtue,
cowardice the greatest vice.
Non-violence springs from love,
cowardice from hate.
Non-violence always suffers,
cowardice
would always inflict suffering.
Perfect non-violence

is the highest bravery.
Non-violent conduct
is never demoralising,
cowardice always is.

1929

Each one has to find his peace
from within.
And peace to be real
must be unaffected
by outside circumstances.

1929

It is man's social nature
which distinguishes him
from the brute creation.
If it is his privilege
to be independent,
it is equally his duty
to be inter-dependent.
Only an arrogant man
will claim
to be independent
of everybody else
and be self-contained.

1929

Healthy discontent
is the prelude to progress.

1929

Manliness consists not in bluff,
bravado or lordliness.
It consists in daring
to do the right
and facing consequences
whether it is in matters social,
political or other.
It consists in deeds,
not in words.

1929

*Commonsense is
the realised sense of proportion.*

1929

Golden fetters
are no less galling
to a self-respecting man
than iron ones;
the sting lies in the fetters,
not in the metal.

1929

It would conduce
to national progress
and save a great deal of time
and trouble
if we cultivated the habit of
never supporting the resolutions
either by speaking
or voting for them
if we had not either
the intention or the ability
to carry them out.

1929

*Breach of promise
is a base surrender of truth.*

1929

Intellect takes us
along in the battle of life
to a certain limit,
but at the crucial moment
it fails us.
Faith transcends reason.
It is when the horizon
is the darkest
and human reason
is beaten down
to the ground
that faith shines brightest
and comes to our rescue.

1929

*I reject
any religious doctrine
that does not
appeal to reason
and is in conflict
with morality.*

1930

Gentleness, self-sacrifice
and generosity
are the exclusive possession
of no one race or religion.

1930

*Each one prays to God
according to his own light.*

1930

The world is touched by sacrifice.
It does not then discriminate
about the merits of a cause.
Not so God—
He is all seeing.

He insists
on the purity of the cause
and on adequate sacrifice thereof.

1930

Breach of promise
is no less an act of insolvency
than a refusal to pay one's debt.

1930

Prayer is not asking.
It is a longing of the soul.
It is daily admission
of one's weakness.
It is better in prayer
to have a heart without words
than words without a heart.

1930

The law of sacrifice is uniform
throughout the world.
To be effective
it demands the sacrifice
of the bravest
and the most spotless.

1930

Man becomes great
exactly in the degree
in which he works
for the welfare
of his fellow-men.

1930

We may have
our private opinions
but why should they be a bar
to the meeting of hearts?

1930

There should be truth
in thought, truth in speech,
and truth in action.
To the man who has realised
this truth in perfection,
nothing else remains to be known
because all knowledge
is necessarily included in it.

1931

*I would heartily welcome
the union of East and West
provided it is not based
on brute force.*

1931

I saw that nations
like individuals
could only be made
through the agony of the Cross
and in no other way.
Joy comes not out of infliction
of pain on others
but out of pain
voluntarily borne by oneself.

1931

An ounce of practice
is worth more
than tons of preaching.

1931

Courage has never been known
to be a matter of muscle;
it is a matter of the heart.
The toughest muscle
has been known
to tremble
before an imaginary fear.

It was the heart
that set the muscle atrembling.

1931

To me art
in order to be truly great must,
like the beauty of Nature,
be universal in its appeal.
It must be simple
in its presentation
and direct in its expression,
like the language of Nature.

1931

God sometimes does try
to the uttermost
those whom
he wishes to bless.

1931

*When restraint and courtesy
are added to strength,
the latter becomes irresistible.*

1931

Suffering
has its well-defined limits.
Suffering can be
both wise and unwise,
and when the limit is reached,
to prolong it
would be not unwise
but the height of folly.

1931

Have I not gazed
at the marvellous mystery
of the starry vault,
hardly ever tiring
of the great panorama?

1931

I have worshipped woman
as the living embodiment
of the spirit of service
and sacrifice.

1933

Proved right should be capable
of being vindicated
by right means
as against the
rude i.e. sanguinary means.
Man may and should shed
his own blood for establishing
what he considers to be his right.
He may not shed the blood
of his opponent
who disputes his 'right'.

1933

I look only to the good qualities
of men.
Not being faultless myself,
I won't presume to probe
into the faults of others.

1933

*Woman
has a compassionate heart
which melts
at the sight of suffering.*

1933

*Everyone who wills can hear
the inner voice.
It is within everyone.*

1933

I have been a willing slave
to this most exacting Master
for more than half a century.
His voice has been
increasingly audible
as years have rolled by.
He has never forsaken me
even in my darkest hour.
He has saved me often
against myself
and left me not a vestige
of independence.
The greater the surrender to Him,
the greater has been my joy.

1933

A certain degree
of physical harmony
and comfort is necessary,
but above a certain level
it becomes a hindrance
instead of a help.

Therefore the ideal
of creating
an unlimited number of wants
and satisfying them
seems to be
a delusion and a snare.

1933

Evil is,
good or truth misplaced.

1933

There is no human institution
but has its dangers.
The greater the institution,
the greater the chances of abuse.
Democracy is a great institution
and therefore it is liable
to be greatly abused.
The remedy therefore is not
avoidance of democracy
but reduction of the
possibility of abuse to a minimum.

1933

Man can never be
a woman's equal
in the spirit of selfless service
with which Nature
has endowed her.

1933

*I believe
in the fundamental truth
of all great religions
of the world.*

1934

My life is one indivisible whole,
and all my activities
run into one another,
and they all have their rise
in my insatiable love of mankind.

1934

I need no inspiration
other than Nature's.
She has never failed me yet.
She mystifies me,
bewilders me,
sends me into ecstasies.
Besides God's handiwork,
does not man's fade
into insignificance?

1934

*The real ornament of woman
is her character,
her purity.*

1934

To deprive a man
of his natural liberty
and to deny to him
the ordinary amenities of life
is worse than starving the body;
it is starvation of the soul
the dweller in the body.

1934

Humility cannot be
an observance by itself.
For, it does not lend itself
to being deliberately practised.
It is, however,
an indispensable test
of 'Ahimsa'.
For one who has 'Ahimsa'
in him it becomes part of
his very nature.

1935

God, as Truth, has been for me
a treasure beyond price.

May He be so
to every one of us.

1935

Non-violence is the greatest force
at the disposal of mankind.
It is mightier than
the mightiest weapon
of destruction devised
by the ingenuity of man.

1935

Destruction is not
the law of humans.
Man lives freely
only by his readiness to die,
if need be,
at the hands of his brother,
never by killing him.
Every murder or other injury,
no matter for what cause,
commited or inflicted on another
is a crime against humanity.

1935

The main purpose of life
is to live rightly,
think rightly,
act rightly.
The soul must languish
when we give all our thought
to the body.

1936

Unwearied ceaseless effort
is the price that must be paid
for turning faith into
a rich infallible experience.

1936

*Manliness consists
in making circumstances
subserve to ourselves.
Those who will not heed
themselves perish.
To understand this principle
is not to be impatient,
not to reproach fate,*

*not to blame others.
He who understands the doctrine
of self-help
blames himself for failure.*

1936

Surely conversion is a matter
between man and his Maker
who alone knows
his creatures' hearts.
A conversion
without a clean heart is,
in my opinion,
a denial of God and Religion.
Conversion
without cleanliness of heart
can only be a matter of sorrow,
not joy, to a godly person.

1936

I have not
the shadow of a doubt that
any man or woman can achieve
what I have,
if he or she would make
the same effort and cultivate
the same hope and faith.
Work without faith
is like an attempt to reach
the bottom of a bottomless pit.

1936

Ill-digested principles are,
if anything,
worse than ill-digested food,
for the latter harms the body
and there is cure for it,
whereas the former ruins the soul
and there is no cure for it.

1937

The essence of all
religions is one.
Only their approaches
are different.

1937

Restraint never ruins one's health.
What ruins it, is not restraint
but outward suppression.
A really self-restrained person
grows every day
from strength to strength
and from peace to more peace.
The very first step
in self-restraint is
the restraint of thoughts.

1937

We should meet abuse
by forbearance.
Human nature is so constituted
that if we take
absolutely no notice
of anger or abuse,
the person indulging in it
will soon weary of it and stop.

1938

True religion
is not a narrow dogma.
It is not external observance.
It is faith in God
and living in the presence of God.
It means faith in a future life,
in truth and Ahimsa.
There prevails today
a sort of apathy towards
these things of the Spirit.

1938

Only he can take great resolves
who has indomitable faith
in God
and has fear of God.

1938

A small body
of determined spirits
fired by an unquenchable faith
in their mission
can alter the course of history.

1938

I may live without air and water,
but not without Him.
You may pluck out my eyes,
but that cannot kill me.
You may chop off my nose
but that will not kill me.
But blast my belief in God,
and I am dead.

1938

Man's nature
is not essentially evil.
Brute nature
has been known to yield
to the influence of love.
You must never despair
of human nature.

1938

*Freedom is never
dear at any price.
It is the breath of life.
What would a man not pay
for living?*

1938

I know, to banish anger
altogether from one's breast
is a difficult task.
It cannot be achieved
through pure personal effort.
It can be done only
by God's grace.

1938

Everyone has faith in God
though
everyone does not know it.
For everyone has faith
in himself
and that multiplied
to the nth degree is God.
The sum total of all that lives
is God.
We may not be God,
but we are of God,
even as a little drop of water
is of the ocean.

1939

There is no one without faults,
not even men of God.
They are men of God
not because they are faultless,
but because they know
their own faults,
they strive against them,
they do not hide them,
and are ever ready
to correct themselves.

1939

Non-violence and cowardice
go ill together.
I can imagine
a fully armed man
to be at heart a coward.
Possession of arms implies
an element of fear,
if not cowardice.
But true non-violence
is an impossibility
without the possession of
unadulterated fearlessness.

1939

Providence
has its appointed hour
for everything.
We cannot command results,
we can only strive.

1939

The hardest metal yields
to sufficient heat.
Even so must the hardest heart
melt before sufficiency
of the heat of non-violence.
And there is no limit
to the capacity of non-violence
to generate heat.

1939

Rights accrue automatically
to him who duly
performs his duties.

In fact the right
to perform one's duties
is the only right
that is worth living for
and dying for.
It covers all legitimate rights.
All the rest is grab
under one guise or another
and contains in it
seed of Himsa.

1939

It is good to see ourselves
as others see us.
Try as we may.
we are never able
to know ourselves
fully as we are,
especially the evil side of us.
This we can do only
if we are not angry
with our critics
but will take in good heart
whatever they might have to say.

1939

Far more indispensable
than food
for the physical body is
spiritual nourishment
for the soul.
One can do without food
for a considerable time,
but a man of the spirit
cannot exist for a single second
without spiritual nourishment.

1939

A dissolute character is
more dissolute in thought
than in deed.
And the same is true of violence.
Our violence in word and deed
is but a feeble echo
of the surging violence
of thought in us.

1939

Democracy must in essence,
therefore,
mean the art and science
of mobilising the entire physical,
economic and spiritual resources
of all the various sections
of the people in the service
of the common good of all.

1939

A principle is a principle.
and in no case
can it be watered down
because of our incapacity
to live it in practice.
We have to strive
to achieve it,
and the striving should be
conscious, deliberate and hard.

1939

*A nation's culture resides
in the hearts and
in the soul of its people.*

1939

Who am I ?
I have no strength
save what God gives me .
I have no authority
over my countrymen
save the pure moral .
If He holds me
to be a pure instrument
for the spread of non-violence
in place of the awful violence
now ruling the earth,

He will give me the strength
and show me the way.
My greatest weapon is
mute prayer.
The cause of peace is
therefore, in God's good hands

1939

I want to see India free
in my life-time.
But God may not consider me
fit enough
to see the dream
of my life fulfilled.
Then I shall quarrel,
not with Him but with
myself.

1940

All compromise
is based on give and take,
but there can be no
give and take on fundamentals.
Any compromise
on mere fundamentals
is a surrender.
For it is all give and no take.

1940

Between husband and wife
there should be no secrets
from one another.
I have a very high opinion
of the marriage tie.
I hold that husband and wife
merge in each other.
They are one in two
or two in one.

1940

It is foolish to think that
by fleeing one can trick
the dread god of death.
Let us treat him
as a beneficent angel
rather than a dread god.
We must face and welcome
him whenever he comes.

1940

It is the law of love
that rules mankind.
Had violence, i.e. hate, ruled us
we should have become extinct
long ago.
And yet, the tragedy of it is that
the so-called civilized men
and nations conduct themselves
as if the basis of society
was violence.

1940

The badge of the violent is
his weapon, spear, sword or rifle.
God is the shield
of the non-violent.

1940

It is unwise to be too sure
of one's own wisdom.
It is healthy to be reminded that
the strongest might weaken
and the wisest might err.

1940

It is through truth & non-violence
that I can have some glimpse
of God.
Truth & non-violence are my God.
They are the obverse and reverse
of the same coin.

1940

Before the throne of the Almighty,
man will be judged
not by his acts
but by his intentions.
For God alone reads our hearts.

1940

Morality which depends upon
the helplessness of
a man or woman
has not much to recommend it.
Morality is rooted
in the purity of our hearts.

1940

An opponent is entitled to
the same regard for his principles
as we would expect others
to have for ours.
Non-violence demands
that we should seek
every opportunity
to win over opponents.

1940

Glory lies in the attempt
to reach one's goal
and not in reaching it.

1942

Just as a man would not cherish
living in a body
other than his own,
so do nations not like to live
under other nations,
however noble and great
the latter may be.

1942

No religion which is narrow
and which cannot satisfy
the test of reason,
will survive the coming
reconstruction of society
in which
the values will have changed
and character,
not possession of wealth, title,
or birth,
will be the test of merit.

1942

How can one be compelled
to accept slavery?
I simply refuse
to do the master's bidding.
He may torture me,
break my bones to atoms
and even kill me.
He will then have my dead body,
not my obedience.
Ultimately, therefore, it is I
who am the victor and not he,
for he has failed in getting me
to do what he wanted done.

1942

Non-violence requires
a double faith,
faith in God
and also faith in man.

Man falls from the pursuit
of the ideal of plain living
and high thinking
the moment he wants to multiply
his daily wants.
Man's happiness really lies
in contentment.

Power invariably elects to go
into the hands of the strong.
That strength may be physical
or of the heart
or, if we do not fight shy
of the word, of the spirit.

Strength of the heart
connotes soul-force.
Let it be remembered that

*physical force is transitory,
even as the body is transitory.
But the power of the spirit
is permanent even as
the spirit is everlasting.*

1942

Truth quenches untruth,
love quenches anger,
self-suffering
quenches violence.
This eternal rule
is a rule not for saints only
but for all.

1942

My work will be finished
if I succeed
in carrying conviction
to the human family,
that every man or woman,
however weak in body,
is the guardian of his or her
self-respect and liberty,
and that this defence prevails,
though the world be
against the individual resister.

1944

Confession of errors
is like a broom
which sweeps away the dirt
and leaves the surface
brighter and clearer.
I feel stronger for confession.

1945

I worship God
as Truth only.
I have not yet found Him,
but I am seeking
after Him

I am prepared to sacrifice
the things dearest to me
in pursuit of this quest.

Even if the sacrifice
demanded my very life,
I hope
I may be prepared to give it.

1947

We do not need
to proselytise
either by our speech
or by our writing.
We can only do so really
with our lives.
Let our lives
be open books
for all to study.

1948

Reprinted 2001

The quotations of Gandhi are
reproduced with kind permission of
Navajivan Trust, Ahmedabad.

Calligraphy, Design and Printing by
All India Press, Pondicherry